ELK GROVE VILLAGE PUBLIC LIBRARY
3 1250 01202 2830

P9-CRE-117

USING MEASURING CUPS

By Abigail B. Roberts

Please visit our website, www.garethstevens.com. For a free color catalog of all our high-quality books, call toll free 1-800-542-2595 or fax 1-877-542-2596.

Cataloging-in-Publication Data

Names: Roberts, Abigail B.
Title: Using measuring cups / Abigail B. Roberts.
Description: New York : Gareth Stevens Publishing, 2018. | Series: Super science tools | Includes index.
Identifiers: ISBN 9781482463972 (pbk.) | ISBN 9781482463996 (library bound) | ISBN 9781482463989 (6 pack)
Subjects: LCSH: Measuring instruments–Juvenile literature. | Units of measurement–Juvenile literature.
Classification: LCC QC100.5 R478 2018 | DDC 681'.2–dc23

Published in 2018 by
Gareth Stevens Publishing
111 East 14th Street, Suite 349
New York, NY 10003

Designer: Laura Bowen
Editor: Therese Shea

Photo credits: Cover, p. 1 Christopher Futcher/E+/Getty Images; pp. 1–24 (series art) T.Sumaetho/Shutterstock.com; p. 5 Ann Worthy/Shutterstock.com; p. 7 Rob Byron/Shutterstock.com; p. 9 M. Unal Ozmen/Shutterstock.com; p. 11 Karramba Production/Shutterstock.com; p. 13 Ariel Skelley/Blend Images/Getty Images; p. 15 bszef/Shutterstock.com; p. 17 UniversalImagesGroup/Getty Images; p. 19 (safety glasses) tankist276/Shutterstock.com; p. 19 (test tubes) Africa Studio/Shutterstock.com; p. 19 (funnel) 5/Shutterstock.com; p. 19 (tongs) peerasak kamngoen/Shutterstock.com; p. 21 (left) Devenorr/Shutterstock.com; p. 21 (right) withGod/Shutterstock.com.

Printed in the United States of America

CPSIA compliance information: Batch #CS17GS: For further information contact Gareth Stevens, New York, New York at 1-800-542-2595.

CONTENTS

Cups and Containers 4

What Is Volume? 8

Kinds of Containers 10

Look Again 14

More Lab Tools 18

Safety in the Lab 20

Glossary 22

For More Information 23

Index 24

Boldface words appear in the glossary.

Cups and Containers

If you help in the kitchen, you've likely used a measuring cup. Maybe you needed 1/2 cup of oil for a cake **recipe**. Adding the exact amount will make the cake taste just right. Measuring is important in baking—and science!

Scientists do **experiments** to find answers to questions. Just like recipes, experiments often need certain amounts of solids and liquids. If the amounts aren't right, the experiment won't work. Scientists use special **containers** to hold and measure liquids.

What Is Volume?

The amount of space a liquid takes up is its volume. Containers with measurements marked on them help us measure the volume of liquids. Some use the volume **units** called cups and ounces. Others use the **metric** units called liters and milliliters.

1/2 LITRE
450 ml
400 ml
350 ml
300 ml
1/4 LITRE
200 ml
150 ml
100 ml
50 ml
1 PINT
18 oz
16 oz
14 oz
12 oz
1/2 PINT
8 oz
6 oz
4 oz
2 oz
milliliters
ounces

Kinds of Containers

Scientists use measuring cups with special names. Containers called beakers are used to measure and mix liquids. Beakers are shaped like a cylinder, or a tube. They have a flat bottom. Glass beakers can hold hot liquids.

beaker
beaker

Scientists often use containers called graduated cylinders. They're very **accurate**. "Graduated" means they're marked with measurement lines. Liquids in these containers are usually measured in milliliters. You might use graduated cylinders in your science lab.

Look Again

There's a special way to measure the volume of a liquid in a graduated cylinder. The liquid's surface across the container isn't a straight line—it's curved. That's because the liquid "sticks" to the container's walls!

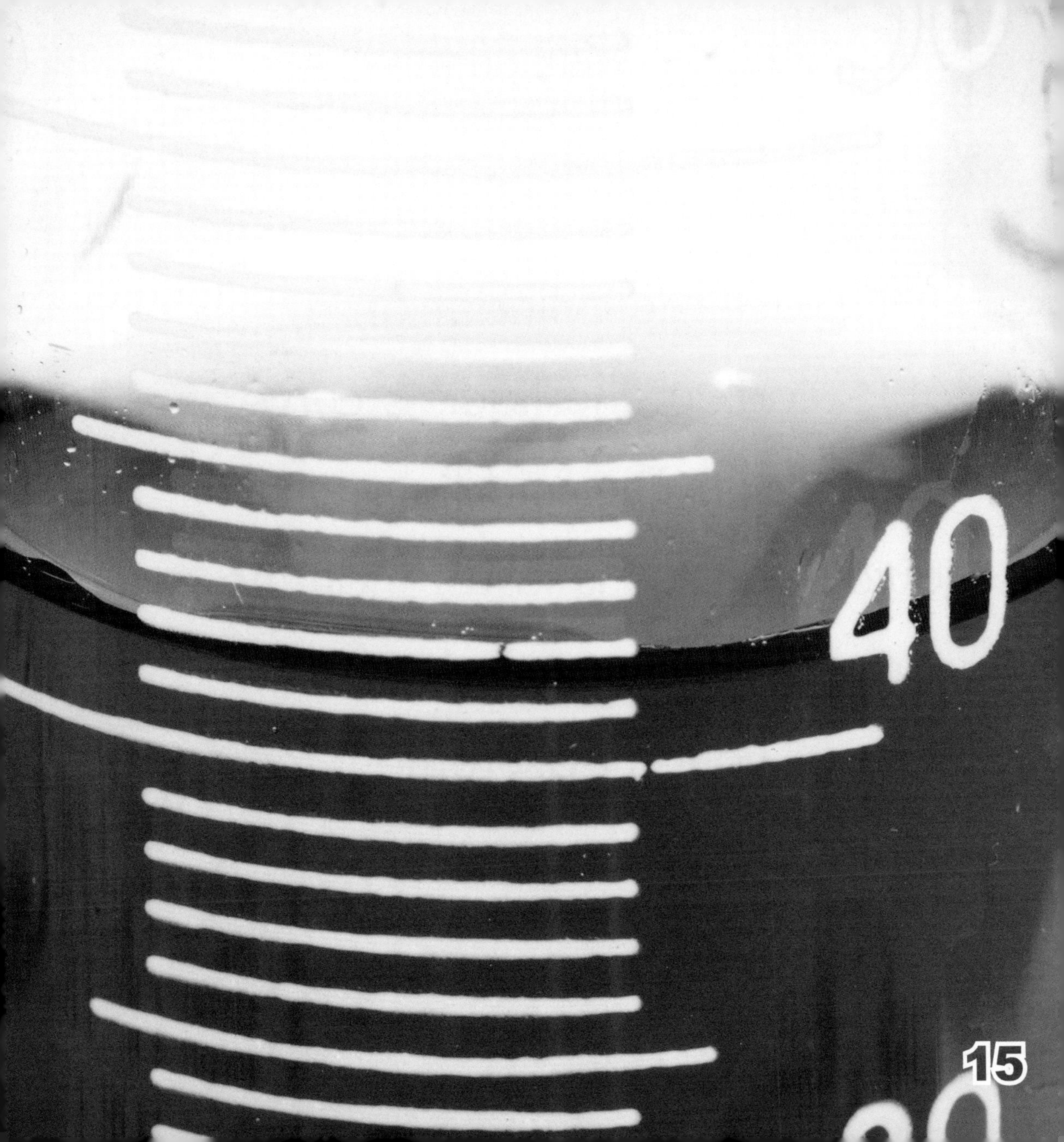
40

First, place the cylinder on a table. Look at the liquid's curve at eye level. The middle of the liquid's surface is lower than the sides. Use the curve's lowest point as your measurement for the liquid's volume.

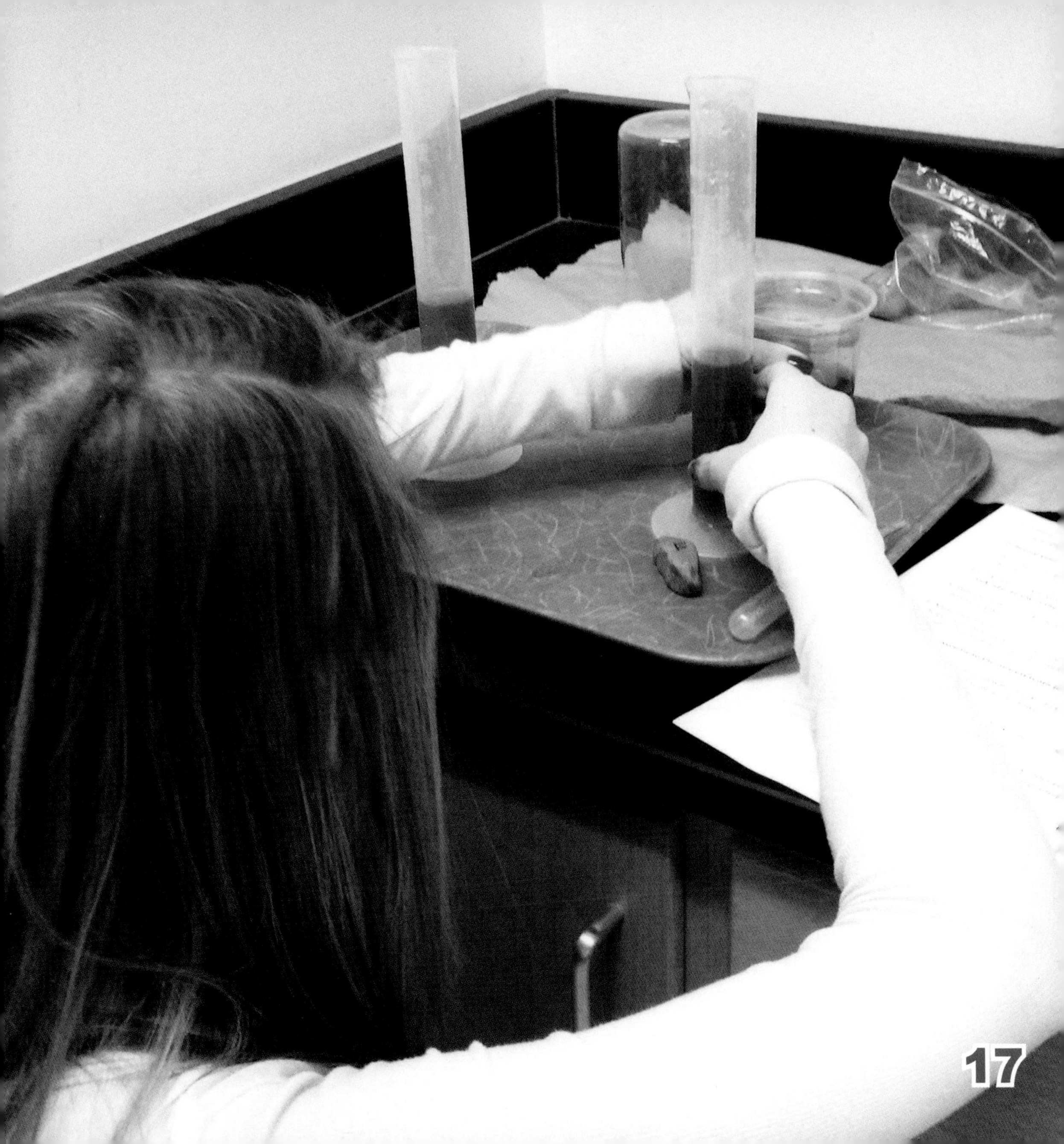

More Lab Tools

Scientists use other tools to handle liquids. **Funnels** help them pour liquids. They use **tongs** to hold hot beakers. Test tubes store small amounts of liquids. Scientists may wear special glasses to guard their eyes from harmful or hot liquids.

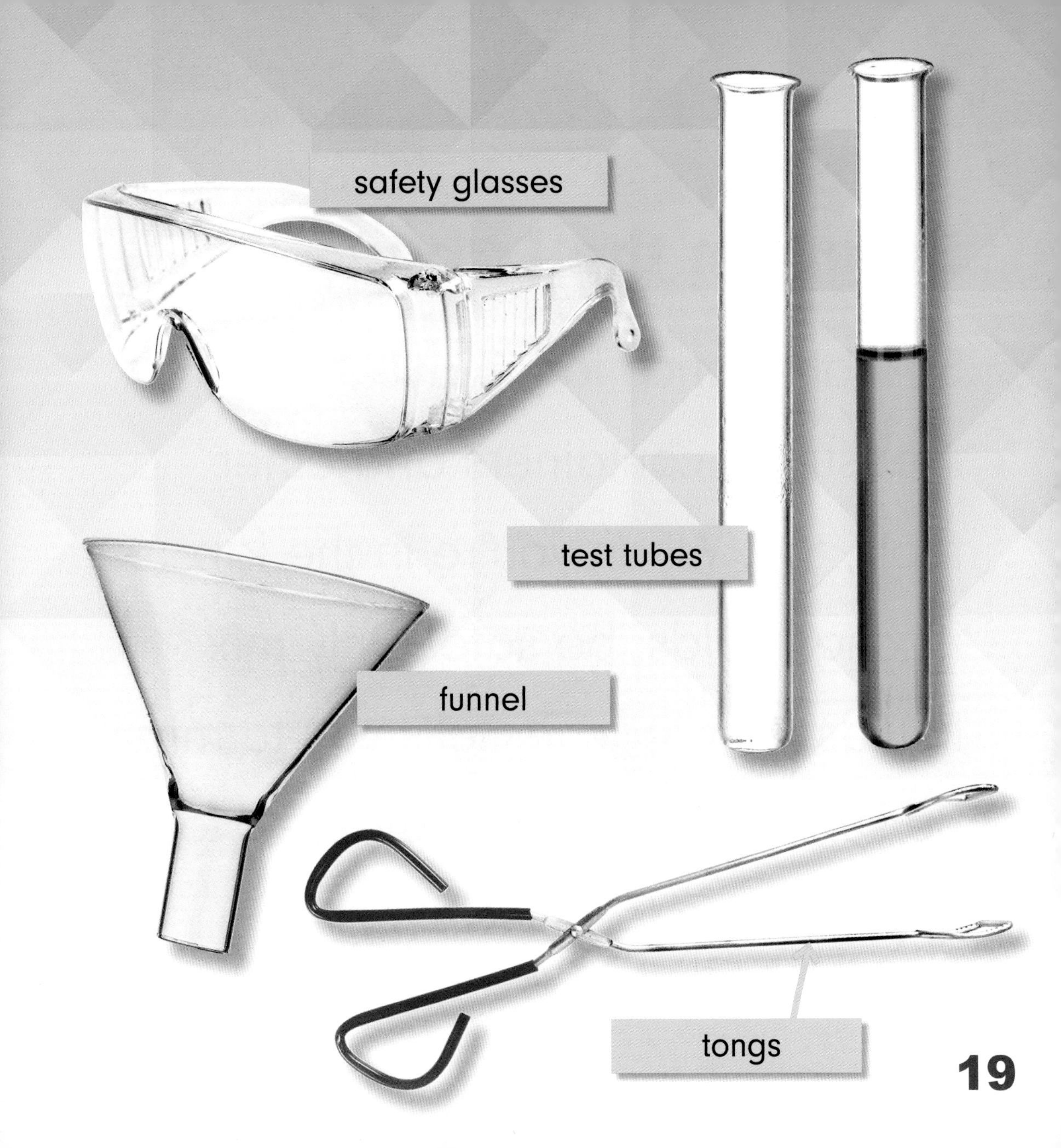
safety glasses
test tubes
funnel
tongs

Safety in the Lab

School science labs have measuring containers and other tools, too. When you're in the lab mixing liquids, be safe. Only mix liquids your teacher tells you to mix. Be sure to wear safety glasses, too. Safe science is fun science!

You Use Measuring Cups!

1) Fill a glass with water.

2) Guess how much water is in it.

3) Use a measuring cup to find out if you're right!

GLOSSARY

accurate: free from mistakes, or exact

container: an object that can hold something

experiment: a scientific test in which you carry out a series of actions and watch what happens in order to learn about something

funnel: a tool shaped like a hollow cone with a tube reaching down from the point

metric: having to do with a system of measurements based on units such as the liter and meter

recipe: an explanation of how to make food

tongs: a tool made of two long pieces used for lifting or holding objects

unit: an amount of length, weight, or volume that is used for counting or measuring

FOR MORE INFORMATION

BOOKS

Lemke, Donald B., and Thomas K. Adamson. *Lessons in Science Safety with Max Axiom, Super Scientist.* Mankato, MN: Capstone Press, 2007.

Reinke, Beth Bence. *Measuring Volume.* Ann Arbor, MI: Cherry Lake Publishing, 2014.

Vogel, Julia. *Measuring Volume.* Mankato, MN: The Child's World, 2013.

WEBSITES

Commonly Used Lab Equipment
teachertech.rice.edu/Participants/louviere/vms/science/labequipment.html
Read simple definitions of science tools.

How to Use a Graduated Cylinder
www.teachervision.com/page/77244.html
Read more about this exact measuring cup.

INDEX

beakers 10, 18

containers 6, 8, 10, 12, 14, 20

cups 4, 8

experiments 6

funnels 18

graduated cylinders 12, 14

liters 8

measurements 8, 12, 16

milliliters 8, 12

ounces 8

recipes 4, 6

safety glasses 18, 20

test tubes 18

tongs 18

units 8

volume 8, 14, 16